This Book
Belongs To:

Easy Planners And Journals
To help you organize your life